Makers of Kenya's History

Alibhai Mulla Jeevanjee

Makers of Kenya's History
SERIES EDITOR: PROF. SIMIYU WANDIBBA

1. *Jomo Kenyatta* - Eric M. Aseka
2. *Ronald Ngala* - Eric M. Aseka
3. *Nabongo Mumia* - Simon Kenyanchui
4. *Dedan Kimathi* - Tabitha Kanogo
5. *Tom Mboya* - Edwin Gimode
6. *Masinde Muliro* - Simiyu Wandibba
7. *Elijah Masinde* - Vincent G. Simiyu
8. *Jaramogi Oginga Odinga* - E.S. Atieno-Odhiambo
9. *J.M. Kariuki* - Simiyu Wandibba
10. *Olonana ole Mbatian* - Peter Ndege
11. *Alibhai Mulla Jeevanjee* - Zarina Patel
12. *Wangu wa Makeri* - Mary W. Wanyoike

Makers of Kenya's History

Alibhai Mulla Jeevanjee

Zarina Patel

EAST AFRICAN EDUCATIONAL PUBLISHERS
Nairobi • Kampala • Dar es Salaam

Published by
East African Educational Publishers Ltd.
Brick Court, Mpaka Road/Woodvale Grove,
Westlands, P.O. Box 45314, Nairobi

East African Educational Publishers Ltd.
P.O. Box 11542, Kampala

Ujuzi Educational Publishers Ltd.
P.O. Box 31647, Kijito Nyama,
Dar es Salaam

© Zarina Patel 2002

First published 2002

ISBN 9966 25 111 1

Cover Illustration by John Nyagah
Photo sections courtesy of Zarina Patel

Printed in Kenya by Fotoform Ltd.
Muthithi House, Muthithi Road, P.O. Box 14681, Nairobi

Dedication

To the Youth of Kenya – the Leaders of Tomorrow

Contents

Preface ix
Acknowledgement xi
Chapter One: Early Life and Travels 1
Chapter Two: Business – The Entrepreneur *Par Excellence* 9
Chapter Three: Politics – From Admiration to Antagonism 16
Chapter Four: Legal Entanglements 36
Chapter Five: Jeevanjee the Man 41
Endnotes 47
Bibliography 48

Preface

'Who was Jeevanjee'? This was the question many asked when 'Jeevanjee Gardens', the only area of refreshing greenery in downtown Nairobi, captured the national headlines in 1991.

Great improvements would accrue, Kenyans were promised. A most modern shopping mall, layer upon layer of parking space – and all underground, out of sight. And to top it all, literally, a concrete piazza complete with glass dome.

And yet hundreds, if not thousands, dug their feet in and said 'Nothing doing.' I was one of them. No way would we let the greedy bulldozers tear up this precious park given to Nairobi so long ago.

Alibhai Mulla Jeevanjee (AMJ), my maternal grandfather, had built it in 1904 and donated it to Nairobians when the city was just a sprawling township. 'He virtually built early Nairobi ... you must write about this', I had been told. But to me wealth and property did not seem enough reason to write a book and I had ignored the proddings.

And then in 1991, the Jeevanjee Gardens saga exploded on to the national scene. My concern for the environment together with my fierce sense of social justice catapulted me into a struggle I had never envisaged. Though the takeover plans had been laid years earlier, the actual battle between the 'developers' and the public raged for two months before the project was halted.

To answer the question, 'Who was Jeevanjee'? I began to delve into his history and stumbled onto the unexpected.

Born in 1856 in Karachi (now in Pakistan) he first came to East Africa in 1890, having spent some years in Australia. AMJ had moved from poverty to riches and then lost it all. He had broken with tradition and ventured across four continents to fulfill his commercial ambitions and become a major pioneer in Kenya. Past middle age he had stepped from a highly successful business career into the world of politics, driven there by the British imperialism that he had once admired and then confronted.

The exploitation AMJ had endured as a boy had left him with a deep hatred of injustice and an unflinching courage to act upon it. In Kenya he provided many services to the British rulers but challenged colonialism in search of a level playing field. He ended up paying dearly for his politics and his family and community compounded to the saga of betrayal.

There are many similarities between his quest for justice and equity and our present-day demands for democracy and basic human rights. The problem of land grabbing persists in Kenya like a cancer in our body politic. A Friends of Jeevanjee Gardens Society has been formed to both protect and up-grade the Gardens. The gazettement of it as a National Monument and the installation of a sculpture of Jeevanjee in it are steps towards the country's recognition of its heroes; this book is another. As we learn more about our past, we are better able to understand the present and plan for the future.

Zarina Patel
September 2001

Alibhai Mulla Jeevanjee (AMJ): Entrepreneur par Excellence

Acknowledgement

The Ford Foundation and the Sir Yusufali Charitable Trust sponsored the initial research for the biography of Alibhai Mulla Jeevanjee. Dana Seidenberg made available to me her collection of cuttings from newspapers published in early 19th century. Terry Hirst and Sharad Shankardass constructively questioned my assumptions and helped me to weave a storyline. Mashengu wa Mwachofi put the historical facts into the perspective of the Kenyan people. They all helped me to know AMJ better and understand the significance of his role in Kenya; my obligation to them is very great.

Many individuals and institutions provided me with relevant information. I cannot mention them all but would like to name a few. Richard Ambani and Peterson Kithuka of the Kenya National Archives got me started on my primary research and Richard Moss showed me maps and photographs of early Nairobi. Dr Barbara Brown, Mahendra Patel, Noordin Tayabali and the late Fidahusein Adamali, Amratlal Raishi, Bachulal Gathani and Hussein Jaffer gave me valuable insights. In India, Salehbhai Badshah invited me to visit his library in Malegaon and Prof. Vijay Gupta assisted me in the Delhi National Archives.

I am grateful to members of the family of Alibhai Mulla Jeevanjee for sharing with me their memorabilia and photographs. To my comrade, Zahid Rajan, I register my deep appreciation for his expertise and his continued care and support.

Chapter One

Early Life and Travels

Alibhai Mulla Jeevanjee (AMJ) was born in 1856 in Karachi in what was then India and is now Pakistan. His family belonged to a Shi'a Islamic sect known as Daudi Bohra[1]. The community was comprised largely of petty shopkeepers who generally have a tendency to be conservative and traditionalist. He grew up in a typical extended family where his parents lived with his father's parents and brothers and their wives and children. This arrangement, often known as the 'joint family system', had economic and cultural functions. It ensured that family members continued to be closely involved in the family business and under the supervision of the oldest male person. It also protected their cultural norms from outside influences, particularly those of Westernisation.

The Jeevanjees resided in a Bohra locality, education was centred on religion and exposure to the outside world was minimal. The family business revolved around horses. Moosajee Mulla Jeevanjee, AMJ's father, owned a horse and cart and made a modest living as a transporter; ironically he was killed by a fall from a horse. He left six young children, AMJ the eldest child and his three brothers, Gulamhusein, Ebrahim and Tayabali, and two sisters, Nemet and Khatija. AMJ now came under the care of his uncles and resented the harsh treatment meted out to him.

It was common in colonial India for sons to travel to distant lands in search of a better living. But being the oldest in the family, AMJ was expected to stay at home, get married and attend to the welfare of the family. Instead, one crucial day, AMJ stole some rupees from under his mother's pillow and escaped from Karachi and thus from the cruelty of his uncles and the conservatism of his environment.

At this time India was colonised by the British and the Empire had spread its tentacles to Africa, Australia and other parts of the globe. It was the age of the Industrial Revolution in Britain, North America had been 'discovered' and the slave trade triangle established. There was a dramatic growth in world trade; it was a time of exploration, adventure and expansion as Europe's merchants spread outwards in search of new markets and raw materials. Here in East Africa, the Omani Arabs had settled in Zanzibar and were joined by the British and Germans. Burton and Speke had set off to find the source of the Nile.

AMJ wandered through India keenly observing the dynamics of a modern society and developing a new consciousness, which transformed him into a bold, out-going and self-confident businessman. He returned to Karachi and, no longer subservient to his uncles, he established A. M. Jeevanjee & Company. Karachi was a port with a well-established shipping industry and the company loaded and off-loaded the visiting vessels (stevedoring) and provided an interpreter for the crew (dubashing).

But British colonialism placed restrictions on Indian entrepreneurs in order to promote industry and employment in Britain. AMJ had heard of far-off lands and exciting trade opportunities, he dreamed of great fortunes and longed to be free and independent. In 1886, leaving his firm in the care of his brothers, he sailed to Australia, landing in Adelaide in the south.

Racism towards non-white people was already prevalent in Australia[2], as it was in the Americas and in Africa, but it was directed more at the Chinese immigrants, as the number of Indians was negligible. AMJ was averse to being employed so he became a peddler, hawking Indian spices and textiles from house to house. Soon he became fluent in English and in the expanding economy, was able to establish an agency for Indian goods.

Meanwhile, his family in Karachi was getting impatient for his return. AMJ was now 30 years old and tradition required that he should have got married much earlier. Leaving his affairs in the care of the uncle who had come to take him back, AMJ left for Karachi but was betrayed by this uncle who immediately thereafter wound up AMJ's business and followed him. In Karachi AMJ was married to 12-year old Jenabai who had been selected as his bride. Child marriage was prevalent in India then so the union did not raise any eyebrows. She was the daughter of Adamjee, a wealthy contractor, so clearly AMJ's family had moved up the class ladder. They now expected him to settle down and apply his knowledge and skill to expand their business even further. But AMJ had other ideas.

In Australia he had met British officials who had become his friends. They had told him about Africa and the great opportunities there for commercial ventures and personal freedom. In Karachi, added to colonial restrictions and Bohra conservatism, was the religious bondage exercised by the sect's High Priest – all these were factors, which led to AMJ's decision to escape again.

In 1890, AMJ left his wife and family and boarded a dhow. This time he was headed westwards to East Africa, in exactly the opposite direction of his previous journey to Australia. A sense of rootlessness and a longing to be free again combined with hopes of limitless opportunity as an Indian in British territory drove him on. The adventure he had embarked on as a young man when he first left Karachi continued.

The route he followed was an ancient one as traders from East Africa and India had been visiting each other's shores for over 2,000 years and possibly more. AMJ set off from Porbandar on the Gujerat coast, a major port of call for dhows from Africa and the Arabian Gulf. The monsoon wind known as the *kaskazi* in East Africa blew southwards from the northeast between December and April and it was in these months that sailing vessels embarked from India on this route. The journey was risky and took over twenty days to complete; AMJ felt a great sense of relief as he sailed into the harbour, now known as Old Port, in Mombasa.

In no time he was down to business. He had good contacts, some capital and a well-established firm in Karachi to back him up. And, as an outcome of his house-to-house hawking in Australia, he was fluent in English, which meant he could establish close relationships with the British directors and officials of the Imperial British East Africa Company (IBEAC). This firm had been developed in 1889 by Sir William Mackinnon, a Scottish shipowner, who had founded the British India Steam Navigation Co[3] in 1872 and was trading with Zanzibar.

AMJ recruited three hundred men from the vicinity of Delhi, India, and supplied them with rations on a three-year contract to police the Company's territory. 'I was entrusted with the Commissariat contract and I was also called upon to supply rations and labour to the Indian contingent under the command of Captain Rogers, which I did', writes AMJ.[4]

In the following year the Company decided to build a narrow-gauge light railway to pass through the thorn bush and past the tsetse fly belt. AMJ supplied the Indian labour which was highly successful in the construction work but the railway project did not get very far as the IBEAC ran short of funds. In 1891, AMJ established a branch of his Karachi-based firm of A. M. Jeevanjee & Co. and started the business of stevedoring and dubashing, the first of its kind on the East African coast. The basic principle in working at the port was to turn a ship around as soon as possible and so economise on charges. Workers were hired on a daily basis and seldom did the same man work two days running as a day's wage was sufficient to keep him for several days. All costs were passed on to the shipping companies so profits for AMJ were assured.

AMJ's experience in Karachi many years earlier proved useful to him and he was now able to provide good, efficient services in both the ports. This facility was of great value to Sir William Mackinnon's shipping line and its agents, Smith Mackenzie & Co. in Mombasa. AMJ continued to service the ships until 1902 when, after the death of Mackenzie, he had some misunderstanding with the management. He then closed down the business and transferred it to Bombay and Marmagoa in India.

A stack of testimonials[5] throws light on the high degree of efficiency and integrity that AMJ maintained in his business dealings. By 1895 a harbour at Kilindini had been developed, some ships were berthing there and goods were being delivered for the construction of the Uganda Railway. Various shipping officials praised the firm for its 'straightforwardness, painstaking energy, punctuality and despatch' and mentioned particularly 'their willingness to work continuously over night as well as day and their safety in handling heavy machinery'.

But port dealings had their intrigues and in Karachi AMJ was faced with a group of stevedores and dubashers who had decided to monopolise the business for themselves. AMJ had the 'audacity' to secure a contract because of its reasonable terms. Standing up for his right to freely compete against the Karachi port mafia was an early signal of what was to become a lifetime campaign for justice and equality.

In 1888, the Imperial British East Africa Company (IBEAC), which was based in Bombay, was given a charter by Queen Victoria to trade in East Africa. In penetrating East Africa, the IBEAC utilized the laws and personnel of the Government of India as well as indentured Indian labour. From 1892 onwards the Indian Penal and Civil Codes applied, and judicial appeals were heard in the Court of Bombay. Indian commercial laws, the Stamp, Inventions, Design and Insolvency Acts were adopted and the Indian rupee was the East African currency until 1920. Hindi words were absorbed into Swahili and East African English. The Indians who settled in East Africa were therefore able to adapt easily to their new country and, not surprisingly, viewed BEA as an extension of India.

The IBEAC, in addition to establishing trading posts all the way to Uganda, had leased a strip sixteen miles wide along the coast from the Sultan of Zanzibar, declared a sort of English protectorate in Witu and built a telegraphic line between Lamu and Mombasa. However, given the deficit of capital in the IBEAC, AMJ began to support the view that the territory should be handed over to the British Government. Obviously he was totally unaware at this time of the broader objectives of British Imperialism.

The primary interest of the IBEAC and the British Government was in the area of Uganda and not Kenya. In 1869 Britain had built the Suez Canal in Egypt in order to secure a shorter passage to India, which was considered to be the most precious jewel in the imperial crown. To ensure control over Egypt it was necessary to control the source of the Nile at Lake Victoria. Frederick D. Lugard, an IBEAC official, was based in Uganda and had to get his supplies from Mombasa. Transport by human porterage and camels had proved unsatisfactory and so a railway was proposed. Hence the name 'Uganda Railway'.

The IBEAC officials travelled to Britain for discussions with their government and AMJ returned to India to pursue his business affairs there.The IBEAC did not have the finances and after a lengthy debate which went on for three years in the British Parliament, the Government decided to undertake the project in 1895 and the IBEAC was wound up.

Thus the British Parliament took over more direct rule of BEA. Zanzibar had already been made a protectorate in 1890 and Uganda in 1893. On 15 June, at a ceremony in Mombasa, the East African Protectorate (EAP) was formally declared. A party of engineers sailed from Britain to start work on the construction of the Uganda Railway and at their request, AMJ joined them at Aden and they all arrived in Mombasa on 12 December 1895. Work started in earnest in January 1896 when the first batch of labourers, who included carpenters, smiths, clerks, surveyors and draughtsmen, arrived from India. AMJ, together with one Hussein Bux, was the major contractor for the recruitment of labour from India. At the time this was the only option as the local Africans, having their own economic structures, were self-sufficient. They were small cultivators and pastoralists who had access to land for which they did not have to pay rent and were settled with their families among their own people. Others were well-to-do traders who travelled abroad. They had no need to become permanent wage labourers.

The labour contract ended in 1900 but AMJ's involvement with the Uganda Railway continued till 1903. The firm of A. M. Jeevanjee was awarded the contract for supplying the workers' rations and other supplies such as timber, wooden beaters, blankets and water bottles. It undertook various jobs such as clearing the bush, arranging the survey of Mombasa Island, building a small quay at the Kilindini harbour and cutting rock and other earthworks. It was also involved in the locomotive department fitting up the rolling stock and building railway wagons for the passenger and goods trains. Out of a total of 37,747 indentured labourers imported from India, 2,493 died in the EAP and 6,724 remained behind by choice. The rest returned to India. Those who remained were joined by increasing numbers of immigrants, mainly from the Punjab and Gujerat areas of India. Most were relatives of those who had stayed. By 1914, the Indians numbered 34,000.

AMJ's first wife, Jenabai, visited the EAP twice and died in Mombasa in 1903 in childbirth. She left behind three children of whom Yusufali, the eldest son, worked closely with AMJ and was of great assistance to him. AMJ's second marriage was to Dayambai who had lost both her mother and her husband at an early age. Living in Bombay, Dayambai was a follower of Mahatma Gandhi. She was well versed in political and religious affairs and is remembered for her concern for the welfare of others. Fiercely independent, she led a very simple life remaining unaffected by the wealth around her and insisted on personally carrying out the household chores and walking rather than being chauffeured. AMJ provided her with residential houses in Karachi and Bombay and she visited the EAP regularly until finally settling here in 1928. She bore AMJ four daughters, Fatam, Sugra, Asma and Shirin, and two sons, Akbar and Asgher.

AMJ's cultural roots were unequivocally Indian. Though he moved with ease in Western society and was, for the greater part of his life, an ardent admirer of British imperialism, he never allowed Western values to impinge on his cultural roots. This is true of most South Asians in Kenya even today. Centuries of tradition bolstered by strong religious beliefs have given them a unique identity, often trapping them in a cultural cocoon. As a result both Africans and Europeans have complained of their isolationist attitude. But AMJ, while rooted in his Eastern traditions, was able to reach out and adapt Western modernity to suit his needs. His clothes had to be well-tailored and laundered and were essentially Indian in style though he would combine his traditional *sherwani* (long coat) with a Western tie and trousers for official functions.

Stockily built, short in height and very round in girth, his handsome face had an air of benevolence and earnestness. Aloof and self-contained, he was tough and hard to ruffle; yet many spoke of his charm and graceful manners. Highly disciplined and very particular about punctuality, he would not tolerate lateness. Victorian in his habits, AMJ was steady, abstemious and methodical but neither prudish nor narrow. Basically a quiet person, he would talk a lot with friends and colleagues but his presence did not inspire intimacy, it was not meant to. He rarely scolded or shouted and commanded considerable respect. His politics brought him into contact with some of the greatest leaders of his time and he was widely travelled and greatly revered. The *Leader* in 1913 wrote that 'of all the Indian prominent men we have met in this country, Mr. Jeevanjee is the first and only with whom one may converse just as one might with a European businessman'.

Chapter Two

Business – Entrepreneur *Par Excellence*

AMJ had an in-born sense of commerce but he was unusual in that money, the end product, was not of primary importance to him. He was most moved by challenges and with his extraordinary courage and foresight, would plunge into the most daunting of projects. During his sojourn in Australia he peddled exotic Indian spices and textiles in two baskets slung from a pole across his shoulders. It is said that whenever the family pressured him about 'getting married', he would respond by saying 'but I have two wives'. As he moved from house to house he soon became fluent in English though he remained largely illiterate all his life. In 1887 he attended a Jubilee Exhibition in celebration of Queen Victoria's 50th birthday and was able to establish an agency for the import of Indian goods in Adelaide.

In 1889, an uncle visited AMJ and was able to persuade him to go to Karachi and get married while he took care of his business for him. AMJ left for Karachi but the uncle soon followed having sold AMJ's business. AMJ got married to Jenabai and the family now expected him to settle down with them and develop the A. M. Jeevanjee & Co. further. But he had other ideas. In Australia he had met with British officials who had told him about East Africa and given him an introduction to B. T. Finch, Superintendent of Telegraphs in Karachi. Finch urged AMJ to travel to East Africa and gave him a letter of introduction to Sir Francis de Winton, Administrator General of the IBEAC. AMJ set sail, this time westwards from Karachi, and landed in Mombasa in 1890.

In the harbour, the Old Port as it is known today, he encountered a maze of sailing ships, fishing boats and dugouts. The island was settled largely with Waswahili and Arabs and about 500 Indians and a sprinkling of Europeans; the Miji Kenda lived further inland and along the coast. AMJ stayed initially with a well-established Bohra family in Ndia Kuu.

The Old Town encircled Fort Jesus built by the Portuguese in 1594. It was walled and was crisscrossed by narrow lanes; there were a few stone houses amongst the mud huts with their *makuti* (coconut leaves) roofs. The rest of the island, apart from a few cultivated areas, was dense bush and wild animals roamed the area. Mombasa was a busy trading port where goods and produce were bartered and from where caravans left for the interior.

Historically these were momentous times. At the Berlin Conference in 1884-5 the European powers had finalised their scramble for Africa. Germany had taken the area to be known as Tanganyika and Britain had claimed the islands of Zanzibar, Pemba and Mafia and the mainland territory now covered by Uganda and Kenya. The slave trade was being abolished because it had become inconsistent with the economic pursuits of the European powers[6] who now needed a settled labour population to develop their new colonies. In addition, the humanitarian sections of their society had begun to raise objections and so they passed the Abolition of Slavery Act. A thriving Arab-Indian-African trade had existed for centuries along the East African Coast; this was now disrupted as British interests began to predominate.

Soon AMJ was down to business. Having recruited 300 men from India for the IBEAC Police Force in 1891, using his experience in the port of Karachi, he established the first stevedoring and dubashing service on the East African coast. Sir William Mackinnon, a director of the IBEAC, had founded a shipping line, the British India Steam Navigation Co. and made much use of AMJ's services.

AMJ also undertook road building and transport, which included importing camels from India and building a 208-kilometre road between

Kibwezi and Kedong on the western border off the EAP. This road facilitated transport by caravan to Uganda and he was able to finish it in record time. He was also requested to look into the possibility of importing Indian agricultural labour into British East Africa (BEA).

The IBEAC planned to build a narrow-gauge railway starting at Mombasa and extending beyond the tsetse fly belt. But after 7 miles, AMJ had to abandon the project as the IBEAC ran out of funds. AMJ viewed his first few years in Africa as 'having done nothing but simply laboured hard at a very heavy loss' and returned to India.

The building of the Uganda Railway started in 1895. AMJ, who had gone back to India, was requested to return and became immediately involved in the recruitment of labour from India and its up-keep. He also took on contracts, which ranged from clearing the bush to off-loading railway stock and supplying various goods and services. He constructed the railway stations, offices and living quarters as well as a quay at the Kilindini harbour.

The Uganda Railway reached Nairobi in 1899 and Port Florence (now Kisumu) in 1901. The expenditure involved meant that the British Government was now constrained about investment for developing the territory and turned to individuals with capital to assist.

AMJ had made a fortune on the railway; his assets in 1900 were estimated at 4 million sterling pounds[7] (an equivalent of 8 billion pounds today). He offered to build structures for the Colonial Administration on the understanding that the land he thus developed would be leased to him for 10 years and an agreed rental would be paid to him during that period. At the end of 10 years the Government would have the option of buying the building or relinquishing the land to AMJ.

John Ainsworth was the first Commissioner of Ukambani Province and Nairobi, still a city of tents, came under his jurisdiction. He accepted AMJ's offer and construction work commenced. Among the buildings erected by AMJ were the following: Ainsworth's house on the site of the present Lecture Hall of the National Museum, Ainsworth's office (now Moi Avenue Primary School), a Town Hall which also served as a court (on the site of the present Imenti House), the Survey Department (the buildings are still standing next to the Central Police Station) and the first Museum (the site of the present Windsor House). In addition, the Government entrusted AMJ with the task of building temporary Government offices, staff quarters and dispensaries between Mombasa and Kisumu as well as police lines, hospitals, post offices and education departments. Other buildings included a mess at Mazeras for the King's African Rifles, a house for a Dr. Stordy in Naivasha, laundry facilities, a kerosene oil store, a slaughterhouse for the municipality and livery stables which were specially requested by Sir Charles Elliot, the first Governor. The buildings were made of wood and corrugated iron sheeting and were built on stilts for insulation from the black cotton soil.

In appreciation of his services, AMJ was given the land between the present University Way and Biashara Street. On it he built the new Indian Bazaar, which was earlier located in a marshy area at the north end of Victoria Street (Tom Mboya Street). He donated part of the land for the allocation of Jeevanjee Gardens and on its west side, built Jeevanjee Market, the only building in Nairobi in 1904 not constructed of iron sheets. Lying between the present Muindi Mbingu and Koinange Streets, the purple and yellow structure had a central clock tower from the balcony of which one could see the snow-capped peaks of Mt Kilimanjaro and Mt Kenya. Prior to this the Municipal Council had planned to erect a market for Europeans only but AMJ built, at the cost of 100,000 Rupees, a market that was accessible to all and which became an outlet for African agricultural produce.

He also had buildings along Victoria Street in Nairobi, McDonald Terrace (Nkrumah Road) and Kilindini in Mombasa, and in Kisumu. In Mombasa he built a most elegant Bohra mosque and a villa for himself, his brothers and their families. AMJ chose to live on the southernmost edge of the Old Town beyond which few would venture because of the fear of wild animals. The house had two storeys and a lookout and was distinguished by a tiled roof with a crenellated wooden border, arched shuttered windows and stained glass. The lounge was so large that a special carpet had to be woven for it in India. The grounds consisted of orchards and gardens and the main trolley line had a branch to the entrance where there was a small hall that the family could use as a cinema. The estate was auctioned in 1935; the villa is still standing but is now in a very dilapidated state.

The villa in Nairobi was situated off Forest Road, was plainer but had 3.2 hectares of orchards and gardens. In the late 1920s when AMJ's wife and children moved to Kenya on a more permanent basis, he bought a four-hectare plot with a large stone bungalow in Second Avenue Parklands, becoming the second Indian family to move into that all-white area. In 1890 in Karachi, AMJ had acquired a princely bungalow for his family residence. Originally built by the British for the nobility, it was a three-storeyed structure with a watchtower and shady garden. The structure still exists though now in poor condition with squatter families occupying it.

Such was the extent of AMJ's properties that in 1904, the *Anglo-African Argus* reported that 'Mr. Alibhai Mulla Jeevanjee, the senior partner of A. M. Jeevanjee & Co., owns about half of Mombasa and the greater part of Nairobi'.

AMJ had worked with horses in his younger days and so, not surprisingly, he became the first person in the EAP to import racehorses from India. He was a keen race-goer and the first race meeting was held in Machakos on 22 June 1897 in honour of Queen Victoria's Jubilee. Rugged Somali ponies were ridden before the horses took over. In 1900 the racecourse was moved to Nairobi, initially to near the Railway quarters and in 1904, to Kariokor at the site of the present Armed Forces base. It remained there until the early fifties when a new course was constructed at Ngong. The road leading to Kariokor is still known as Racecourse Road and the area on the Ngara side of it is marked as 'Jeevanjee Estate'. Though AMJ's horses did well at the races, AMJ became increasingly uncomfortable with the racist attitudes of the Settlers and in 1906, withdrew from racing.

AMJ's businesses included ice and soda factories and import and export of agricultural and industrial products. He was a shrewd businessman and ruthless when crossed. When the owner of the *East Africa and Uganda Mail* tried to grab AMJ's contract for supplying oil to the Railway, AMJ bought out the total supply of oil on the market and eventually sold it to the Railway at twice the original price. Palmer, the owner, took AMJ to court alleging fraud and the case became the subject of a Supreme Court hearing but the judge ruled that AMJ was entitled to the price he had named.

The *Mail* covered the 'Castor Oil Saga' word-for-word and after losing the case took on an increasingly anti-Indian tone. In response, AMJ established his own newspaper – the *African Standard*, the forerunner of our *East African Standard (EAS)*. Never one to do things in halves, AMJ imported the first high-speed press in the EAP and recruited William Tiller from London as editor. The press was housed in a building opposite the Old Law Courts in Mombasa. A veritable war of words ensued with the *Mail* becoming increasingly abusive and insulting and Tiller bringing criminal and libel charges against the editor and publisher. As the *Mail* became more and more filled with gossip, important government and commercial news began to be solely published in the *Standard*. In 1904 the *Mail* was declared bankrupt and the following year, AMJ sold the *Standard* to Anderson and Mayer who established the *EAS* - one of Kenya's major newspapers today.

At this point AMJ's heart was in India and his main concern was business, not politics. He must have hoped that the new owners of his newspaper would continue to steer a moderate course and this was the case initially. But soon the editorial policy of the *EAS* succumbed to the dictates of Lord Delamere and his cronies and for the next sixty years the paper consistently voiced the interests of the Settlers. One of the clauses of the sale contract was that nothing derogatory to AMJ would ever be published by the *EAS* and this explains why in the ensuing years when AMJ became a fiery antagonist of the Settlers, the *EAS* carried no articles critical of him. The worst it could do was to deny him coverage. AMJ with his astute foresight had foreseen the future scenario and taken the necessary precautions.

In 1910, a pro-Settler newspaper described AMJ as a 'hustler' and went on to state that he was 'a real asset to a young country'. AMJ used his contacts and his service abilities to the maximum and took well-calculated risks with confidence, favouring business propositions of an original and pioneering character. A pragmatist, he responded to challenges with reasoned arguments and well-thought-out projects. The hustler was in fact an entrepreneur of significant magnitude and it was not surprising that his success generated praise, as well as antagonism.

Chapter Three

Politics – From Admiration to Antagonism

After the Berlin Conference of 1884-5 when Britain acquired control of territories in East Africa, the Imperial Government began to encourage Indians to emigrate to East Africa in order to service the labour, administrative and commercial needs of the EAP. The railway workers who remained were joined by their relatives and associates. Utilizing family support and backed by their ethics of hard work and frugal living, the Indians were able to spread out into the most remote areas of Kenya and to delve into trade, masonry, agriculture and the administrative and service sectors.

Earlier in 1900, a Mombasa Indian Association had been formed by L. M. Savle in order to assist new immigrants from India. The Settlers who were largely from the British aristocracy were unable to compete against the Indians and began to resent them. Racial discrimination became the most appropriate weapon to use in the fight for control as they could then appeal to the authorities on the basis of 'kith and kin'. In January 1902, twenty-two Europeans formed a Colonists Association and appointed Lord Delamere as their leader with the purpose of discouraging Indian immigration and fostering white settlement.

AMJ joined the Mombasa Indian Association and together with Allidina Visram, began to agitate for Indian rights. In 1906, a branch was opened in Nairobi under the presidency of Visram and in 1907 a

British East Africa Indian Association was formed as an umbrella body. AMJ's interest was commerce, not politics but as he stated later, 'I felt very keenly the humiliating condition of my fellow-countrymen, I could not bear to see with philosophical calmness the unequal and unjustifiable treatment meted out to them by the white population of East Africa'. In 1906, the seat of government was moved from Mombasa to Nairobi and steps were taken to constitute a parliament – both these moves favoured European interests, as Nairobi was the hub of the Settler population. Liberal sentiments still prevailed and Churchill urged the appointment of an Indian to the parliament to represent 'this large and meritorious class'. In the same year, as president of the Mombasa Indian Association, AMJ transformed it into an organisation fighting for equal rights and justice.

Disillusioned with Settler intransigence, AMJ at this time was spending more time in India. However, in 1909 his name, at the insistence of the Colonial Office, was put forward as the best-qualified Indian representative for the Legislative Council (Legco). AMJ returned, most reluctantly, to take up his position in March. He was only too well aware of the racial hostility he would encounter in the Council apart from the fact that he would have to sacrifice his businesses in India. But Indian leaders both in East Africa and India urged him to take up the appointment, as it was the first time that an Indian had been nominated to a parliament in a British colony.

The absolute impossibility of the Indians receiving a fair hearing, added to the fact that AMJ was illiterate in the English language, made his attendance in the Council an exercise in futility. Rather than face constant humiliation and antagonism, he decided to table Indian grievances directly to the Colonial Office in England and travelled there in July. This was by no means his first visit to Britain; he knew many friends and well-wishers. He was hosted by the Eastern Question Association and interviewed by the press. AMJ stated that 'a deliberate attempt is being made to debar us from any share in the commerce and agriculture in the country. We are marked down because of our race and colour and yet...no less than 85 percent of the trade is in the hands of the Indians...the proportion of Indians to Europeans is as twelve to one...they pay the whole of the taxes'. He enumerated the instances of discrimination in the sale of produce and the purchase of land, on the Lake Victoria steamers, the inequities of the Emigration Act and the injustice in the courts.

London's *Daily Chronicle* published a series of articles and an editorial in the first week of September and at least eight other newspapers took up the cry. The headlines are indicative of the wave of sympathy in Britain for the plight of the Indians. "Indians in East Africa – Amazing Action of the Colonial Office – Suicidal Policy, No Indian Need Apply, East Africa Policy of Exclusion, More Hindu Grievances, Debarred from Magistracy and Trial by Jury". The articles attracted widespread attention.

Back in the EAP the Settlers were enraged and the *Leader* wrote of 'The Jeevanjee Escapade' and 'His latest taradiddle!' Governor Girouard dismissed AMJ as a 'low caste coolie' and declared that 'this colony is going to be controlled by our kith and kin'. In spite of such hostility, AMJ still considered himself 'a loyal subject of the King and was proud to be a citizen of the British Empire'. Faced by such blatant discrimination and sensing a downturn in the Colonial Office, AMJ in desperation proposed that the EAP be ruled from India. The India Office, he felt, would be more sympathetic than the Colonial Office. The India Office, which of course was also a colonial entity, did take up the matter but the Colonial Office introduced the concept of 'native paramountcy'. This tactic was a red herring and was used again most effectively 10 years later in the *Devonshire Declaration.*

The census at the end of 1911 showed a population of 2,750,170 Africans, 11,886 Indians and 3,175 Europeans in the EAP. Yet the principle of 'one white man, one vote' was being campaigned for. The Settlers demanded that the 99-year leases on their land be extended to 999 years, that the land demarcated for the African reserves be included as Crown Land and that Africans and Asiatics be excluded from owning land in the Highlands. AMJ raised objections on a variety of issues such as the poll tax and the Uganda Cotton Rules of 1913.

On 7 March 1914, together with Allidina Visram, Shrinivas Thakur, L. M. Savle and his wife and Keshavlal Dwivedi, he founded the East African Indian National Congress (EAINC), which incorporated all the Indian Associations and had AMJ as its president. Modelled on the Indian National Congress, it raised, among its first demands, election to both legislative and municipal councils on a common roll. Other main topics of contention by the Indians were the exclusion from the Highlands, denial of trial by jury, prohibition from carrying of firearms and discrimination on the railway and steamers and in the Nairobi public market.

The First World War was declared in August 1914 and following in the footsteps of their political seniors in India, the Indians of the EAP gave their support to the war effort. But the initial enthusiasm of the Indians was soon dampened by the discriminatory attitude of the Europeans. The Indians were placed under close surveillance and African young men were forced to join the carrier corps (hence the name 'Kariokor'). Lewis Walter Ritch, a European lawyer who was sympathetic to the Indians, was arrested and deported without trial. Late in 1915 a small group of Indians was arrested on charges of sedition and anti-British behaviour. They were members of the Hindustan Ghadr Party, a revolutionary movement that had its origins in the 1857 mutiny in India. In May 1916, following a court martial, three were shot, two hanged and eight imprisoned. Savle and Dwiwedi of the EAINC were among those imprisoned. One other was fined and twenty were deported.

The War ended. The colonized peoples who had made significant contributions and sacrifices in the battle for Britain's victory were left with nothing to celebrate. In fact, they were reduced to the position of a conquered race. World War I brought about a qualitative change in the political format of the British Empire. The colonized now had high expectations of a just reward as their basic human right but on the other hand the Settlers, drunk with victory, became even more arrogantly racist. The Crown Lands Ordinance declaring the Highlands as 'white' was passed and plans to demolish the Nairobi Indian Bazaar, enforce municipal segregation and restrict Indian immigration were proposed.

For a while the Indians, hoping to acquire an alternative to the racist antagonism of the Settlers, supported a campaign led by the Aga Khan to make German East Africa a sphere of special Indian interests. This idea, however, never took off the ground.

The most ominous action taken by the Colonial Office was the appointment of Major-General Northey as Governor. This military man was imbued with strong anti-Indian prejudices. In his opening speech on 24 February 1919 he charged that the majority of Indians were not qualified to vote in this or any other country. In April, the Legco restricted the franchise to adults of 'pure European descent'. At a later date Northey stated that 'European interests must be paramount throughout the Protectorate'. Much of the slander against the Indians emanated from a group of Britons whose decadent lifestyle and criminal activities were notorious. They came to be known as the 'Happy Valley Set'.

The immediate post-war years were a critical time for the Indians and a younger group of leaders emerged, most of the old guard having either died or dropped out. Only AMJ continued to take part in active politics.[8]

Most notable among the new leadership was Manilal Desai who had arrived in Nairobi to be a lawyer's clerk in 1915 at the age of thirty-six. A brilliant organizer, he soon invigorated the Indian political structure and through helping Harry Thuku to build his anti-colonial movement, forged links with African political activists. AMJ provided Desai with free living quarters and other assistance to enable him to devote his energies to the political struggle. Such was the communal harmony in those times that he did this in spite of the fact that Desai was a Hindu and he himself was a Muslim. Shanti Pandit, author of *The Indians in East Africa*, wrote 'the house of Jeevanjee was the home for late Mr. M. A. Desai and every political memorandum was mooted and drafted in the busy offices of Messrs A. M. Jeevanjee & Co'.

In January 1919, Lord Milner took over as Secretary of State in the Colonial Office. His racist attitudes soon became evident and hence in March, AMJ led a delegation to India with a list of Indian grievances. It was presented to the Viceroy with a request that it be forwarded to the British cabinet and the Imperial War Conference.

Dayambai, second wife of A.M. Jeevanjee

AMJ strikes a pose of confidence during his heyday

Jeevanjee Villa, Mombasa

Jeevanjee Market, Nairobi

Meeting of Governors and Officials of East and Central Africa, 1927
From left to right; Seated: *Hon. Lady Grigg, AMJ, H.E. Sir Edward Grigg (Governor and the commander-in-chief of the Colony and Protectorate of Kenya), Lady Stanley, Mr. T.M. Jeevanjee* **Standing:** *H.E. Sir William Gowers (Governor, Uganda Protectorate), H.E. Sir Charles Bowring (Governor of Nyasaland), His worship the mayor (Coucillor Ridell) of Nairobi and mayoress (Miss Ridell), H.E. Sir Herbert Stanley (Governor of Northern Rhodesia), Mr. Husseinbhai Suleman Virjee, Mr. C.E. Lyall (Chief Sec. to the Government of Sudan)*

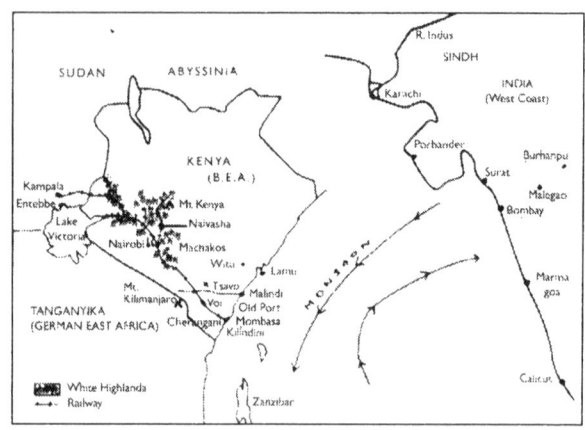

Illustrative map of places visited by AMJ in BEA and India

In addition to the earlier-stated items, the memorandum deplored the absence of Indian representation on the various organs that determined their lives. It was received favourably by the Government of India, noting that the Protectorate Governors were unduly influenced by the Settlers and missionaries and that in 1887 the Consul General in Zanzibar had stated that '... drive away the Indian and you may shut up the protectorate'. A report on the memorandum asked 'What would be said of a person who was helped by a friend in time of need but who, as soon as he got out of his difficulty, told his benefactor that he had no obligations towards the latter because his help was no longer needed'?

Meanwhile in the EAP in June 1919 the Settlers drew up a set of demands that they termed the 'Irreducible Minimum'[9].

It consisted of five points:

1. Residential and commercial segregation;

2. Exclusion of Indians from the Highlands;

3. A maximum of two nominated Indians on the Legco;

4. Restrictions on Indian immigration; and

5. Full recognition of existing Asiatic rights in property and security of tenure. [inserted to placate the Indians]

Further intrusions on Indian rights were a proposed bill in Legco to regulate shop hours and the non-recognition of professional degrees conferred by the British in India.

A 'divide and rule' policy was now activated. In August a Mr. V. V. Phadke was nominated to the Legco. The Indians were campaigning for 'electoral' representation and the Indian Associations in BEA stated that they viewed the acceptance of the seat by Mr. Phadke with 'great disapproval'. Another side of this policy was to pit Indians versus Africans. An article in the *Leader's* 6 September 1919 issue read '... the Indian[s] ... deprives the African of all incentives to ambition and opportunities of advancement'.

The EAINC protested vigorously about all the injustices and innuendos. When Indians were prohibited from bidding for sixty Nairobi business plots, the EAINC appointed AMJ to lead a delegation of three prominent Indians to meet with Milner in London in March 1920. This time he took with him his wife, Dayambai, and youngest child, Shirin.

Representatives from the Indian Overseas Association and the Indian National Congress joined the delegates. They met with the Colonial Office (CO) and the India Office and put forward their claim for 'equality' not 'preference'. They justified it on the basis of their numerical majority vis-à-vis the Europeans, their greater capital investments, larger contributions to taxes and value as skilled labour and the fact that the Protectorate's laws, currency and administration were modelled on those of India.

The CO had to accept the fact that 'East Africa cannot at its present state of development do without the Indians' but veered towards a policy of 'protecting the African'. Thus were sown the seeds of the colonial doctrine of 'African Paramountcy' that was finally adopted in 1923.

AMJ expressed his profound disappointment 'at the failure of His Majesty's Government to deal with them with even-handed justice'. He now became nostalgic about the pre-1895 years when the welfare of the Indian communities in BEA came under the jurisdiction of the India Office and Indians were treated with a measure of respect and care and suggested 'the transfer of this Indian colony from the jurisdiction of the CO to that of the Indian Government'. Another delegation sent by the EAINC to India was concerned with Indian settlement in German East Africa. Gandhi in Bombay rejected both notions as being 'imperialistic'.

On 23 July 1920 the British Government formally annexed the EAP and renamed it Kenya Colony and Protectorate (the latter referring to the coastal strip leased from the Sultan of Zanzibar). Following the meeting with the AMJ deputation, Milner and Northey, who was then in England, worked out a solution to what had become known as 'the Indian Question'. The Settlers were calling for a denial of the franchise to Indians and for their ultimate exclusion from the Protectorate. The Indians, on the other hand, were agitating for equal rights and full representation. The CO was manouvering in a thorny situation. Contrary to expectations, the solution elicited an immediate outcry among the

Kenya Indians and in India at the 'inferior status assigned to British Indians in Kenya'.

The Indians were aware that without an adequate voice in the highest decision-making body they did not stand a chance of influencing laws and policies in their favour. 'Two representatives cannot adequately voice the views of 22,000 Indians if it required eleven members to voice the views of 8,000 Europeans', they insisted and resolved to boycott all public bodies. Abdul Rasool Visram resigned his Legco seat on 25 November and Phadke followed suit in January when the legislature passed a motion upholding segregation. Meanwhile Gandhi had already declared that 'the British Government was ruling India by deceit', and called for non-cooperation. On the other hand, the *EAS* referred to the speech as 'seditious' and Delamere resigned from Legco in protest at the unrestricted immigration of Indians into Kenya.

AMJ was still in England at the request of the EAINC, which fully approved the work he had done and the policies he had adopted while there. 'All East Africa Indians will stand by you to the end', the EAINC cabled him. In October he left for India where he consulted with Gandhi and other Indian National Congress leaders before sailing to Kenya in November. Lalchand Sharma, who was one of the persons jailed for sedition by the British, was a fellow traveller. His diary notes refer to AMJ's thorough knowledge of business, particularly concerning land property and his political acumen. 'In spite of not having enough knowledge of the English language he kept fighting for Indian rights', he writes. 'Seth A. M. Jeevanjee kept inviting me to take lunch with him and I must express my thanks to this great man'. This note gives an insight into AMJ's character.

The SS Karagola docked in Mombasa on 27 November 1920 and AMJ disembarked to preside over the third session of the EAINC. This was truly a memorable meeting, with the BEA Indians united in their determination to fight for their rights and their refusal to settle for anything less. Mombasa was decked out for the occasion and delegates streamed in from East Africa and India. Governor Northey, however, declined to open the session, preferring to attend the Nakuru Show, which was being held at the same time.

AMJ's presidential speech[10] was a memorable one of extraordinary length. He left no holds barred as he rose to 'consider a situation in which our very existence as a community is at stake and to take the decisions which concern the honour and self-respect of our race and motherland'. He spoke of the contribution of the Indians to the construction, trade and administration of the colony and went on to analyse the areas in which Indians were being unjustly discriminated against. In doing so he touched on the franchise, land, segregation, racial prejudice, immigration, education and the currency regulations. He demanded equal representation, rejected the idea of a communal franchise but advocated the protection of minority rights. Later in closing his speech he assured the natives and Arabs of his loyal support and solidarity in their struggle to better their positions and emphasized that while the Indians sought to protect their own rights, they did not seek to deny those of others.

After listing various demands and establishing a fund-raising mechanism to finance Congress activities, the EAINC resolved that in the event of a failure of a positive response to their appeal, it would have no alternative but to 'advise and adopt such measures of peaceful and effective political weapons in self defence such as "non-cooperation" to achieve their objects'.

AMJ's scathing denunciation of British colonial policy in Kenya and his strident call for non-cooperation are interesting developments in his political ideology. Settler racism and Imperial hypocrisy fuelled by the events of the First World War had moved him from 'admiration' to 'confrontation'. Throwing caution to the winds even to the extent of neglecting his business and family affairs, he went full steam ahead into the battle for justice and equality. Already his business interests were being threatened by family feuds and the Bohra High Priest had excommunicated him and his family.

The Congress delegates left Mombasa by special train. The *EAS* printed the entire text of the President's speech headlining it in large bold letters as 'Jeevanjee's Speech' and stressed 'the necessity of an early and close study of the Indian problem and the need for a policy of exclusion or accommodation'.

AMJ travelled to Nairobi arriving on the 19th to a tumultuous welcome. At the railway station when he entered a horse-drawn carriage for a ceremonial ride through the streets of Nairobi, the Indians removed the horses and pulled the carriage themselves all the way from the station to Jeevanjee Villa. A newspaper report commented that 'He loved the Indian community and they loved him ... no leader has ever been given so much respect by the masses'.

The year 1921 witnessed a dramatic increase in the hostility of the Settlers towards the Indians. The post-war Depression was hitting the economy, Northey and the Settlers, in order to safe-guard their interests, had instituted forced labour, various taxes and agricultural laws primarily directed at the African population. This caused peasant production to drop and a subsequent collapse of commodity prices.

In the CO, Winston Churchill replaced Milner. This change raised the hopes of the Indians considerably in their quest for justice and fair play as they, and especially AMJ, had not forgotten Churchill's support for them in earlier times.

In Kenya, the situation was worsening. In the Legco abusive descriptions of the Indian community were voiced and a bill providing for commercial and residential segregation in the townships was passed. Phadke, the only Indian member, resigned in protest. The Settlers' manipulation of the currency as they strove to replace the rupee with the shilling as well as benefit themselves in the process, ruined the African peasants as well as many of the Indian traders.

The Europeans stepped up their efforts to drive a wedge between the Asians and the Africans using the growing rivalry between emerging African businessmen and the Indians. 'Educated Natives' wrote in a Ugandan monthly deploring the presence of the Indians. The Young Baganda Association and others refuted this. A telegram sent to the British Prime Minister on 13 July 1921 by Harry Thuku read: 'Native mass meeting held on Sunday 10th. Over two thousand Natives present declared Indians presence not prejudicial to Native advancement as alleged by Convention of Associations. Next to Missionaries Indians our best friends'[11].

Meantime, differences of opinion were coming to the fore within the Indian community. Being by and large business orientated, there were those who did not support political activities. In addition, the call for non-cooperation was viewed as 'extremist' and a threat to their economic survival. Later a two-sided struggle did develop within the Indian political organisations pitting 'moderates' versus 'radicals'. A divergence of opinion was also developing between the Settlers and the CO. Delamere launched his Reform Party on 24 May 1921 with the stated policy of 'stern opposition to the present claims of the Indians'.

Earlier in May, the Indian Association led by AMJ had met with the Convention of Associations for a round table conference to resolve the differences between the two communities. The meeting was held in Government House and Northey presided. Land ownership, segregation, common franchise and taxation were the contentious issues and, after three days of acrimonious deliberation, no agreement was reached on any of them.

On 15 May 1921, at a mass meeting of Indians, AMJ declared the principle of 'No taxation without representation'. It was also agreed to withhold payment of the rates to the Municipal Council as a protest against neglect of services to areas occupied by Indians. Legal wrangles ensued with AMJ as the chief litigant.

Churchill, on the other hand, at the Imperial Conference held in June said 'The British Empire could have only one ideal on this matter, namely, that there should be no barrier of race, colour or creed preventing any man by merit from reaching any station if he were fitted therefore'[12]. He appeared to be genuinely committed to upholding the principles of justice and basic human rights and the Indians now put their faith in the CO. Northey was scheduled to visit London in June and the EAINC arranged for AMJ to lead a delegation to arrive there at the same time. The meeting authorised the AMJ deputation to present the African case and added 'The Natives obtain the opportunity of learning from them [Indians] all kinds of skilled work ... and are guided and shown every sympathy'.

The Indians had helped the militant young Thuku in forming the East African Association. Thuku had established his headquarters in Desai's East African Chronicle office and the press printed his broadsheet, *Tangazo*. The Settlers became alarmed at this Indo-African political solidarity and tried various approaches to undermine it. The bogey of 'communism' was raised and on one occasion a gathering of Indian leaders at which Thuku was present was highlighted in the press as the 'Jeevanjee Tea party' and roundly condemned. AMJ, however, had left the country two weeks prior to this social gathering.

Hysteria seemed to grip the Settlers. They tried to influence deliberations in Britain and began to talk of taking up arms. Highly emotional appeals for funds were made 'likening the 'cunning Oriental' to 'this evil menace now spreading and strengthening its tentacles'. The Christian faith was seen to be at risk and the East Africa Women's League, an association of colonial white women, implored Queen Mary to 'protect us and our children from the terrible Asiatic menace that threatens to overwhelm us'. Horrific visions of 'European women under Asiatic administration', 'Indians flooding the colony' and 'mixed marriages' were some of the scenarios vividly perpetrated. They even accused AMJ of 'bringing out white women to Kenya', a charge which AMJ's manager termed as 'defamatory remarks absolutely without foundation'.

In Britain AMJ was accompanied by Varma, the secretary of the EAINC and representatives of the Indians Overseas Association. Churchill, having met with Northey, received the Indian delegation. He had already accepted the Settlers' demand for segregation in the Highlands and tried to placate the Indians by offering them another area equivalent in size and from which the Europeans would be excluded. AMJ and Varma rejected the offer as 'a breach of the principle of equal citizenship', Churchill's betrayal of Kenya's Indians went even further when he denied the Indian claim of having developed the country saying that it was white capital, brains and science that had done it.

During July and August the Settlers had recruited the nucleus of a secret army and Churchill succumbed to the threat of a European revolution in Kenya. He made some interim proposals and left it to Northey and the EAINC to work out the details. Varma returned to Kenya with Northey while AMJ, at the request of the EAINC, stayed on to facilitate representation to the CO. AMJ urged his EAINC colleagues to work for unity with the Arabs and the Natives. 'The

Europeans will not be able to stand if we all combine against them', he wrote. He also advised the EAINC to elect Varma or Desai to the presidency at its next session as 'matters will be very political and we shall need a strong man in the chair'.

In September, Desai with great foresight predicted that 'the coming problem of the Colony is the native problem' and warned, 'When they are fully awake, well just look out'[13].

In December, Delamere led a deputation to London financed by the Convention. The EAINC wired its acceptance of the interim proposals but unknown to them, Churchill had already abandoned the proposals stating 'there will be no radical changes before February 1923'.

He even decided to eventually amalgamate Kenya, Uganda, Tanganyika and Zanzibar and confirmed his turn-about by declaring that Kenya was to become 'a characteristically and distinctively British Colony'.

Needless to say, Indians everywhere bitterly resented Churchill's pronouncements. AMJ vowed that Indians in all the four territories 'will by every constitutional means oppose a territorial amalgamation'. The anger and alarm were felt by leaders in India, by Harry Thuku and other African nationalists in Kenya and by the Anti-Slavery Society in England. The Settlers, on the other hand, were on the warpath, threatening revolution and urging a boycott of Indian shops. In February 1921, playing a cat-and-mouse game, Churchill accepted to meet with the AMJ delegation. It was a stormy meeting with AMJ accusing Churchill of perfidy. The EAINC in Kenya, however, buoyed by this contact, dropped its plans for non-cooperation and renewed its acceptance of some of the interim measures.

In December 1921 he had pleaded with the EAINC to send somebody to take his place as 'I have now been over here a very long time'. However, the EAINC requested that he remain in Britain and AMJ acceded, obeying orders and trusting that matters would soon be settled. After the meeting with Churchill, AMJ travelled to India to attend to his family and business affairs which had been severely neglected. The EAINC wrote to him saying, 'we trust that you will do all you can in India. We wanted you here [in Kenya] very badly now but unfortunately your business will not allow you to be absent from India'.

In Kenya Harry Thuku was mobilising the African masses around the issues of land, a living wage and an end to forced labour. Struggling to contain Indian demands, the Kenya Government became alarmed at the rising tide of African militancy and its close association with the Indians. On 22 March 1922, Thuku was arrested. The next day a large crowd which had gathered to demand his release, was shot at and the official toll was 23 killed and 27 wounded. Desai's *East African Chronicle*, which supported Thuku, was punished with crippling libel damages and was forced to close.

Leaders in India expressed strong resentment and called for equality in Kenya. Churchill must have been perturbed and he took the unusual step of replacing Northey with Sir Robert Coryndon as the new governor of Kenya. In October, Churchill lost his seat in Parliament and was himself replaced, as Secretary of State for the Colonies, by the Duke of Devonshire. The latter locked horns with the Settlers who in turn attempted a trade boycott and stepped up their plans for a revolt.

The situation was volatile. AMJ in India submitted a request to the Indian Government for arms and an army contingent. In February 1923, in a debate on the Indian Question in the British House of Commons, it was moved that 'this committee is of the opinion that there is no justification for assigning to Indians in Kenya a status in any way inferior to any other class of His Majesty's subjects'[14]. An explosive confrontation was avoided and Coryndon allowed the Indians as well as the Settlers to send deputations to England at public expense.

The long-drawn out feud between Kenya's Indians and Europeans had reached a critical stage. All concerned were aware that the planned negotiations in London would be decisive, not just for the protagonists but for the country as a whole. On either side the contingents were large and impressive, Delamere brought along two Maasai men; Desai led the EAINC leaders which included AMJ, leaders from India and the Aga Khan and Polak who were in London.

The Delamere group's main objective was to secure European self-government while the Indians wanted equality. None of the protagonists, least of all the Europeans, were at this point primarily concerned about the rights of the Africans. The European delegation received backing from both the press in England and Smuts from South Africa and Indian leaders alleged that 'it was accorded favoured treatment by the CO'. Churchill meanwhile continued to give evasive and even false information in the House of Commons. Kenya's Indians felt trapped and strove as best they could.

The White Paper, entitled *Indians in Kenya: Memorandum* and better known as the *Devonshire Declaration*, was published on 25 July 1923, the Delamere group having received it thirty-six hours earlier. After stating that Kenya was primarily an African country and confirming the doctrine of native paramountcy, it detailed future policy regarding the Indian problem. On the Legco there were to be eleven Europeans (elected), five Indians (also elected) and two Arabs (one elected and one nominated). A missionary would be appointed to represent African interests. The communal franchise was to remain. Segregation in the towns was abandoned but restrictions on immigration were to be imposed. The Highlands were to remain exclusively 'white'.

The Settlers' threats of rebellion had succeeded. The Indians were dismayed. Sastri from India termed it as a blow to the moderates. His famous phrase 'Kenya lost – all lost' summed it all. In India the doubting Thomases now embraced Gandhi's call for *swaraj* (independence). The stage was set for a worldwide struggle between white and coloured peoples[15].

Kenya's Europeans, while winning the battle for short-term white supremacy, had lost the war for self-government. The country was saved from the extreme tyranny of apartheid or going the independent way of Australia, New Zealand or Canada. The declaration of African paramountcy in the Devonshire's White Paper, though not implemented, ensured that in major decisions affecting the colony, the interests of the majority superseded those of the minority.

AMJ had stayed on in England awaiting the outcome of the elections to be held in January 1924. The British Labour Party took over from the Conservatives and this change raised the hopes of the Indians. AMJ wrote to the EAINC leaders 'to sever all connections with the Europeans, both in trade and service', and urged all Indians to keep unity. The EAINC meanwhile had resolved to suspend payment of the Poll Tax by Indians in Kenya and in February several of its leaders were charged and imprisoned for default in payment of taxes.

AMJ expressed surprise at the Kenya Government's actions – jail in a civil case, which was distinctly political, seemed unwarranted to say the least. He wanted the Indians to engage in even more forceful protests but that was not to be. His fervour and absolute commitment to the cause of justice were not widely shared. Kenya's Indians were tiring of the long and seemingly unending confrontation. Worse still, their fragile unity was being severely tested. The Indians consisted of a diversity of religions, languages and occupations and their numbers had now reached a point when exclusive communal organizations had become viable. Opposing class interests too, were beginning to become entrenched and the British 'divide and rule' policy further strained this unity.

But most crucial of all was the economic hardship the Indians were undergoing. The boycott of Indian merchants and artisans, a wholesale expulsion of Indian railway employees with a reduction in wages for the remaining ones and a similar policy in the private sector – all these broke the back of Indian resistance. The tax boycott petered out at the end of March without any tangible results having been achieved.

In November 1924 the Labour Party was voted out of office having been of no significant benefit to the Kenya Indians. AMJ refused to give up the fight. He identified an Indian barrister in England who could represent the EAINC there on political matters but his suggestion was not taken up. He wrote to various Government authorities in England and India explaining the situation and asking for support but to no avail. The leaders in India were now preoccupied with their own struggle against imperialist oppression and hence their attention was shifting away from Kenya. The Kenya Indians began to accept the status quo but did not relinquish their objections to the Devonshire Declaration. They refused to have anything to do with the communal franchise; only 200 names were entered into the voters' register, which was open to 15,000 Indian men and women.

In Britain, the Conservatives appointed Amery, a staunch imperialist, as Secretary of State for the Colonies and Sir Edward Grigg, an outright pro-European, as Governor of Kenya. Both were committed to building BEA into a great white dominion and thus European, not native, paramountcy was their goal. And the Indians were considered a liability to these plans. They were not just ignored, they were victimised. Exclusion from a public auction of plots in Mombasa, an increase in the Asiatic Poll Tax, marginalisation of Indians in the municipal councils and Grigg's cooperation with Delamere to foster closer union of the East African territories – all these new onslaughts against the Indians goaded them into action. They withdrew their participation in the legislative and municipal councils and re-instituted the policy of non-cooperation.

A notable development in this period was the process of class formation taking place within the Indian community; ethnic chauvinism began to be used to promote class interests. Compromise, not non-cooperation was advocated and a splinter group favouring closer cooperation with the Government broke away from the EAINC.

In 1926, in an attempt to heal the emerging rift, the EAINC called on AMJ again to lead them. At seventy years of age and in failing health, he assumed the presidency taking over from Sarojini Naidu. His presidential address was nowhere near as fiery or lengthy as the one he had given in 1920; it dealt more with the immediate past, leaving the strategies for the future to be mapped out by the members themselves. But his conviction and determination regarding justice, equality and basic human rights remained as principled and strong as ever.

Referring to the rival Indian Association that had been set up in Mombasa, AMJ decried the first serious split in the community in the decades of hard struggle put up by Kenya's Indians. On the attempts being made for Closer Union of the BEA territories, AMJ termed them as South African methods, which would be to the detriment of Indian citizens. Manipulation of statistics and discriminatory taxation were other anti-Indian tactics, which needed to be countered.

Six years lay between AMJ's two presidential addresses; the EAINC was meeting in December in Mombasa again but a new era had begun in Kenya's history. The struggle of Kenya's Indians which had dominated the political scene for a quarter of a century was not only being superseded by African nationalism but was also itself taking a new and different direction. The *Devonshire Declaration* had been the turning point. Markedly absent from AMJ's address was any reference to India or the tactics of non-cooperation. Nor was there any mention of equality or rights. His emphasis was on the economic needs of the Indians and he studiously avoided the contentious issues that divided the Congress delegates.

The issue of the common roll was a high priority and after protracted deliberations, the EAINC opted to accept the communal roll under protest and provisionally only. In March 1927 AMJ travelled to London and made one last attempt to reason with the CO but the latter was clearly not interested. Having won over the moderate Indian leaders, the CO, in league with the Kenya Government, was now all set to rule the colony in the interests of their kith and kin and to try and keep the nascent African nationalism at bay.

In July 1926, AMJ's protégé Desai, an outstanding Indian leader, brilliant organizer and staunch anti-imperialist, had contracted typhoid and died near Bukoba, Tanganyika. He was on a mission to raise funds for the *East African Chronicle*. In order to fill the gap and to inject more radicalism into the Indian political struggle, AMJ brought out Isher Dass from England in 1927 to act as his private secretary. Dass became a formidable champion of African and Indian rights and was the first Indian to support the African cause with revolutionary ideals[16].

There was a great deal of dissatisfaction among Kenya's Indians regarding the resolutions of the 1926 EAINC session, especially the one which accepted the communal roll, and political agitation was vigorously renewed. While AMJ presided at political and social functions he seemed increasingly to be playing more of a background role. And then in July 1927, he suddenly resigned from the presidency of the EAINC, though he continued to serve as Acting Vice-President until 1931.

At this time he was in severe financial difficulties and was being harassed on several fronts. He was in the vortex of family feuds, religious persecution and colonial injustice but nevertheless continued to give the Indians his fatherly guidance. 'Place self-respect above everything', 'issues should be properly discussed and debated', 'self-help was the key to success' – these were some of his words of wisdom. He was adamantly opposed to the policy of 'Closer Union' and disagreed with the representatives from India who urged the EAINC to relinquish the idea of a common roll.

AMJ's wife and children visited him regularly from India. In 1928, AMJ bought a large estate with a bungalow in Nairobi at Second Avenue, Parklands and moved them permanently to Kenya. The house still stands but is now located in a densely built up estate. Though AMJ dropped out of circulation, his advice was constantly sought and notable visitors would make their way to him. One of these was General Smuts whom AMJ had got to know when he visited Gandhi in South Africa. The colonial government tried to dissuade Smuts from meeting AMJ but was not successful.

Colonial vengeance was now directed at AMJ and in 1931, in the Imperial Government's birthday honour's list, it was his brother and not him who was awarded the Most Excellent Order of the British Empire (O.B.E.). And a newspaper correspondent noted that 'there are some who will say that a British title for an Indian is no honour'. Years later in 1950, when Nairobi became a city, AMJ's role in the building of the town did not even get a mention in the Nairobi Jubilee Booklet.

Notwithstanding his life-long crusade against racism, AMJ held no personal rancour or hatred and maintained good relations with his white contemporaries. In April 1921, in spite of the breakdown of the Nairobi Round Table Conference and Northey's partisan behaviour, he gave a magnificent garden-party as a farewell to Lady Northey. He entertained H. E. Sir Edward Grigg and Lady Grigg and in 1927, the Governors and Officials of East and Central Africa.

AMJ's commercial empire included offices in Karachi, Bombay, London and Berlin. Shortly after the end of World War 1 he tried to establish direct commercial relations between Germany and India for his firm but was not successful. His interest in shipping dated back to the 1880's when A. M. Jeevanjee & Co was established to service ships in the port of Karachi. He acquired a number of steamers and a fleet of native craft, which sailed between Indian and Arabian ports. In 1920 he bought four steamers of 5,000 tons each for the use of passenger and cargo trade between Mombasa and Bombay. To do this he drew a lump sum of 100,000 sterling pounds from his bank[17].

Reporting this, a newspaper article described AMJ as 'the merchant prince of Kenya'.

The EAINC had on several occasions discussed the 'atrocious service of the British India Steam Navigation Co. to non-whites' so the demand for transport was indisputable. And yet AMJ's shipping venture ended in disaster! Two of the ships, SS Nairobi (which the Government used to transport Harry Thuku to his detention in Kismayu) and SS Calicut ran aground the Kenyan coast in 1923. At the time the Government had disallowed an enquiry into the matter stating that the ships were registered in Bombay and were the concern of the Government of India.

However, five years later, the SS Calicut did become the subject of a commission of enquiry[18] and the record reveals information which points to probable sabotage by the British. In a confidential note to Grigg, Amery, the Secretary of State for the Colonies, stated 'I do not consider that any useful purpose would be served by validating, by legislation, the enquiry which was held in Mombasa'.

For AMJ this misfortune was the 'last straw' – it heralded a downturn from which he was never to recover. He became increasingly embroiled in the claims being made by his family, creditors and mortgagees and this was in addition to the legal battles for titles to his properties. These titles accrued from the agreements made with the early administrators and which the Colonial Government later reneged on. A personal blow was the death of one of his daughters in Karachi, followed by the deaths of her husband and only child six months later. Increasingly he took a backseat in the political arena and, finally, in 1927 resigned from the presidency of the EAINC. He was an intensely private person so his feelings at this time remain unknown.

Chapter Four

Legal Entanglements

AMJ's aggressive business methods together with the Settlers' opposition to him brought him into conflict with the law on several occasions. His first encounter with the law was in India in 1896 when he was recruiting labour for the construction of the Uganda Railway. He had contravened an amendment to the Indian Emigration Act, intentionally or otherwise, and this led to the discontinuation of this particular venture.

In BEA his first brush with the law was in 1899 when one of his trolleys carrying a European woman passenger collided with a handcart in Mombasa. Later in 1901, Palmer, who owned the *East Africa Uganda Mail* newspaper, schemed to grab the contract for supplying lubricating oil to the Railways from A. M. Jeevanjee & Co. AMJ was away in India but he instructed his firm to purchase all the available oil in the market. He then sold it to the Railways at a handsome profit. The Castor Oil Saga became the subject of a Supreme Court hearing in Mombasa, fraud was alleged but the case was dismissed.

In 1906 he had a further altercation with the Protector of Immigrants in India but it was in BEA that AMJ's major legal problems arose – and persisted to the time of his death. At the turn of the century, the local administrators relied heavily on AMJ to build Nairobi. At that time there was no Land Office or Survey Department in existence; growth was spontaneous and town planning only started in 1915.

AMJ in robe presented to him by the Aga Khan

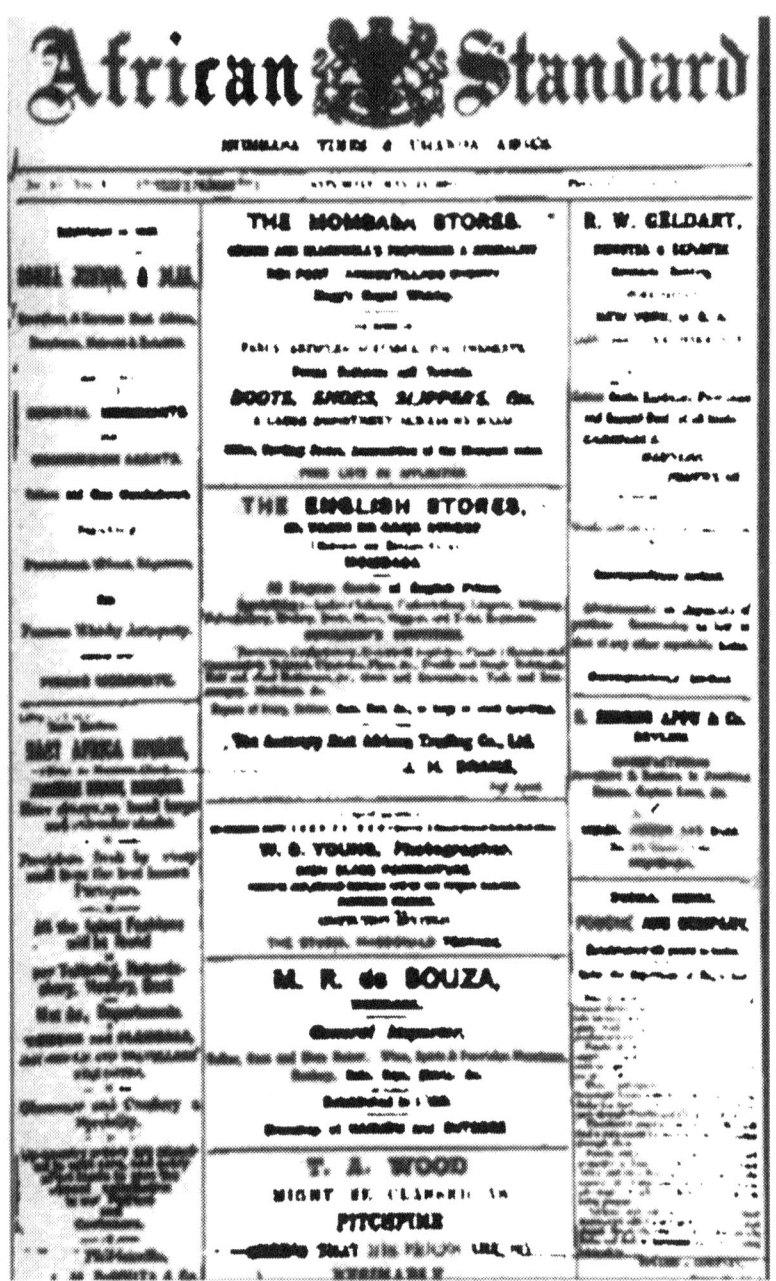

A sample copy of the African Standard, forerunner of present-day East African Standard (EAS)

Unveiling of Queen Victoria's Statue, Jeevanjee Gardens, 1906

Queen Victoria's statue at Jeevanjee Gardens, Nairobi

A recent statue of AMJ at the Jeevanjee Gardens, Nairobi. It was unveiled in May 2001 by His Worship the Mayor of Nairobi, John Ndirangu

AMJ constructed buildings for the Government on a 99-year lease, the first ten years rent-free and thereafter at a rent of 2 rupees per month per building with the option of purchase by the municipality at its original value. In 1903 he built Jeevanjee Market off Muindi Mbingu Street and directly opposite Jeevanjee Gardens. The negotiation with Ainsworth was that a lease of 99 years would be given free of land tax and no other market would be allowed in town. He built the Town Hall-cum-Courthouse at the site of the present Imenti House and other buildings under the same conditions.

Already in December 1904, AMJ was writing to the Nairobi Town Clerk: 'Hoping you will act according to our original mutual agreements'. A year later, Ainsworth recommended that the Government set aside a sum for the purchase of AMJ's houses in Nairobi. 'The present arrangements with Messrs A. M. Jeevanjee & Co. are far from advantageous to the Government. They were however the best that could be made at the time', he explained.

In August 1906, Ainsworth was transferred to Naivasha. The Settlers rejoiced, as they could not stand 'His policy and attitude particularly with regard to the Indian question'. It was a time when men like Ewart S. Grogan were stating that 'Colour distinction was the base of every British social system which comprises various races'[19]. But even this die-hard racist had to accept the tremendous importance of the Indian to the development of East Africa and cautioned, 'Wild abuse of the Indian however will never help us, he is an invaluable, nay, an indispensable factor in our cosmos'.

Having gained dominance of the Nairobi Town Council, the Settlers now began to quibble and question AMJ's rights to the properties he had developed for the Government. This in spite of the fact that they, including Lord Delamere, had been given vast tracts of territory for no service at all! In 1913 Ainsworth, who was stationed in Kisumu, submitted a memorandum to the CO at its request. His conclusion was: 'I do not think even now that a settlement of the present difficulty is a question of money. I think it has more to do with the idea that certain rights are being denied and as a consequence the firm [A. M. Jeevanjee & Co.] feels that they are being subjected to injustice'.

Ainsworth's recommendations were over-ruled and in 1915, AMJ was refused leases for his Market and Stable plots, and changes were introduced in the agreements. The Land Officer was instructed by the Municipal Committee 'not to divulge the contents [of the files concerning the Jeevanjee sites] to AMJ's solicitors. Regarding his Bazaar properties, AMJ was willing to dispose of them if it was in the public interest but stated that he would resist any attempt to deprive him of his property by force.

In 1920 AMJ brought the Market issue to the CO in London for settlement and appealed to Churchill because, as he wrote, 'I have no confidence of this being handled in Nairobi. Unfortunately the part I have taken in fighting [for] my community's rights in the colony has prejudiced the European population'. Meanwhile, in November 1920, J. A. E. Elliott, then District Commissioner in Embu, had alerted the CO about Northey's racist attitudes towards Africans and Indians.

Governor Northey failed to respond to several inquiries from the CO and then in 1922 said 'There was never any agreement to give Mr. Jeevanjee a lease ... there is nothing to show that Jeevanjee was put in possession of the land'. As a final act of intransigence he declared, 'other alternatives were open to Jeevanjee. He could remove the building'. The matter dragged on till 1925 when AMJ, who was in financial difficulties, offered to sell the sites to the Government for 20,000 pounds. The offer was accepted and the payment was made in August.

This was, however, by no means the end of the matter. Problems regarding conditions of contract and ownership of other sites and buildings continued to plague AMJ. One such case concerned a plot of land in Mombasa that AMJ had purchased in 1905 and for which he was being refused a certificate of title. The case was heard in the High Court. In 1916 AMJ took it to the Court of Appeal of Eastern Africa and ultimately to the Privy Council in England. The outcome is unknown.

On 15 May 1921, at a mass meeting of Indians, AMJ had proposed 'no taxation without representation'. In 1922, the Nairobi Municipal Council took AMJ to the Supreme Court 'seeking to recover Sh.12,000 as rates from Messrs A. M. Jeevanjee & Co.' – the entire matter became known as the 'Recovery of Rates Cases'[20]. AMJ's keen mind had noticed a flaw in the Nairobi Ordinance governing the rating of unimproved site values and in September 1923, the Court had no alternative but to dismiss the suit. Messrs Daly & Phadke represented AMJ while Mr. Kaplan was the counsel for the Council.

In July 1924, a new bill had to be drafted by the Attorney General and presented to the Legco to facilitate the collection of municipal rates in Nairobi. AMJ's challenges to the colonial system were principled and astute, and therefore, formidable. It is hardly surprising that the colonial administrators and the Settlers developed such animosity towards him.

The period between 1918 and 1925 was one of extreme confrontation between the Indians and the Settlers and of the Indians' growing disillusionment with the CO in London. Various ruses, including outright bribery, were used to undermine the Indians. Most acrimonious and distressful of all AMJ's legal battles were those that arose from the family feud.

A. M. Jeevanjee & Co. followed the usual mode of an Indian joint family concern in which the oldest male member held authoritative powers. As early as 1918, his youngest brother Tayabali began to question these powers as well as the partnership arrangements and resorted to legal aid. The wrangles dragged on until 1923, the year of the Devonshire Declaration and the year AMJ's ships met with disaster. It was then that AMJ became aware that he did not have sufficient property to pay his debts in full. He could have offset the loss by selling off some of the Karachi properties but was unable to get the necessary consent from his brothers.

In Kenya, unable to get a fair hearing on the matter, AMJ withdrew from the partnership in 1927. Later, in his absence, all the Jeevanjee plots were transferred to the Company. In India the Company properties were mortgaged with the Punjab National Bank holding the judicial lien on them. AMJ travelled to India in 1931 to try and unravel the intricate knot of family, creditors and mortgages but could not get any cooperation from his brothers. He suffered a heart attack and was laid up for several months. The first auction of the plots in Kenya took place in June 1935 - the court brokers were G. A. Datoo in Mombasa and Jamal Pirbhai in Nairobi.

AMJ turned to the courts in his struggle for justice and equal rights but British colonial justice was not as impartial as he believed it to be. This saga of legal entanglements highlights AMJ's tenacity and perseverance and his absolute refusal to compromise with unfair discrimination. The financial empire AMJ had built with his remarkable entrepreneurship was ultimately destroyed by a combination of internecine family quarrels and British colonial injustice.

Chapter Five

Jeevanjee the Man

AMJ died on 2 May 1936 in Nairobi at the age of 80 after a heart attack. His wife, Dayambai, and his sons, Akbar and Asgher, were by his side. He was buried the same day according to Islamic rites in the cemetery plot, which he had donated, at Gikomba. A large gathering of people from all communities attended the funeral but the colonial government made no official acknowledgement of the event.

Though a magnate, at one time owning property worth over 4,000,000 sterling pounds at the turn of the century, this 'merchant prince' died a relatively poor man, leaving his wife and children propertyless. Nevertheless, all the shops in Bazaar Street and businesses elsewhere were closed on the day after his funeral. The residents of Mombasa, under the auspices of the Indian Association, mourned his death at a mass meeting. Newspaper editors paid tribute to him as a great pioneer and articles praising his achievements appeared in the *EAS*, the *Kenya Daily Mail* and the *Coast Guardian*.

Streets were named after him. After independence these were changed to become the present Mfangano Street in Nairobi and Mwagogo Street in Mombasa. But the area between Park Road and Ring Road Ngara, next to Racecourse Road, is still marked as 'Jeevanjee' on the city map.

The *Kenya Daily Mail* obituary, in recording the sense of immense loss, referred to him as 'The Grand Old Man of Kenya' and wrote:

> Indians in East Africa lost a great pioneer...for nearly two decades his masterful personality dominated the Indian public life in almost all activities, but more especially in the politics of the period...It is to his pioneering courage and foresight that Indians in Kenya are today in a far better position than in any other colony or Protectorate of the British Empire.

It went on to describe him as:

> Not a man of much education or fine words, but having indomitable courage and will power which gave him confidence and strength to express opinions freely and without fear of anybody...it was this courage and frankness which had made him a respected and honoured leader of the Indian community.

The *Coast Guardian* remembered him as 'a man of ripe experience, marvellous virility and breadth of vision'. Many years later, in independent Kenya, the *Sunday Post* wrote, 'Jeevanjee deserves to be honoured as the man who awakened the people of Kenya. He was the first man to demand equality. He laid the foundations of an organized political movement'.

Indians had played a merchant role in East Africa's coastal enclaves for centuries. Even today, the major impact of Kenya's South Asians is in the field of commerce and industry where they continue to make a vital contribution. Jeevanjee, however, was the first Indian in East Africa to enter into politics, to confront the Settlers and to pressure Britain's CO for the rights of all Kenyans. He used his wealth, his tireless energy and steadfast determination to pursue this goal. In the process he developed Kenya's first nationally organized political movement, the East Africa Indian National Congress, which inspired both Indians and Africans to continue the anti-colonial struggle.

AMJ's generous nature was evident in the various philanthropic activities he undertook and, in spite of his busy schedule, he showed a real concern for his fellow humans and assisted people regardless of caste or creed. His financial generosity was naturally extended to the political struggle he had inadvertently entered.

AMJ liked to live well. He entertained lavishly and was renowned for his hospitality. His palatial residences in Mombasa and Nairobi were open to a variety of events and peoples and in the absence of any community hall or theatre at the turn of the century, Jeevanjee Villa in Mombasa served as one.

Newly arrived immigrants were helped to settle. Finance and accommodation were readily provided and beneficiaries ranged from socio-religious bodies, sports clubs and the arts. The villas were host to wedding and farewell parties and visiting and local dignitaries, as well as those who were not allowed to stay in the good hotels because of the colour bar. They included Winston Churchill, Sarojini Naidu, Maulana Shaukat Ali, Kunwar Maharaj Singh, the Aga Khan, General Smuts, governors, mayors and other officials in BEA. During the War AMJ placed his spacious house and grounds in Karachi at the disposal of the Government nurses and equipped two wards in Nairobi.

Aside from his political commitments, business activities and travel, he took interest in local social issues and this included, among others, cotton growing in Uganda, the supply of electric power in Mombasa and freight and landing fees charged by the Conference Shipping Companies to African ports. He combined the traditional with the modern and was always willing to learn from new experiences.

The family never saw him lose his temper but his intense seriousness and busy schedule made it difficult for them to relate closely to him. He did not, or could not, share with them his political and business concerns and he often did not give them the attention they needed, but he was a loyal husband and father. Nor were all his interests of a serious nature. Jeevanjee, who had grown up with horses, was a keen race-goer. An accident while playing polo left him with a limp and hence he always carried a walking stick. He would travel to Tanga for a game of bridge with his friends, was one of the first in Kenya to own a car and later a yacht, and was a regular fan of the movies.

Of particular concern to him was the area of education, perhaps because he himself had lacked formal education. Thus it was that at the end of the nineteenth century, he was supporting two *madrassas* (religious schools) in Karachi. In 1901, a Madrassa Hakimia for boys was established in Burhanpur, India. AMJ became involved in its management and lobbied for the inclusion of English and other secular subjects in the curriculum. This brought him in conflict with the Bohra priesthood, which was averse to the broadening of knowledge amongst its followers.

Increasingly AMJ allied himself more closely to the reformists who were demanding accountability and transparency from the religious leaders[21.] In 1917, the reformists took the High Priest to court in Bombay accusing him of theft of community funds and AMJ was one of the witnesses. In the Chandabhai Gulla case the reformists won a major legal victory but as a result were subjected to intense harassment and persecution. AMJ's family became a target; the children had to be removed from school and his wife was abused in public.

This was the main reason for AMJ's decision to relocate his family permanently from India to Kenya where religious intolerance had not yet taken root in his community. But it was only a matter of time and today, over sixty years after his death, many Bohras in East Africa consider AMJ a renegade and most of his family members are reformists. And yet, though he travelled far from the land of his religious forbears, hobnobbed with his peers in the Western world and was surely one of the most cosmopolitan Bohras of his time, AMJ remained a deeply religious man all his life. He prayed regularly and observed the basic tenets of Islam. Though he entertained governors and visiting dignitaries lavishly and with the greatest of pomp, he adhered strictly to his beliefs and would not allow alcohol to be served at any function hosted by him. In spite of the immense wealth he once controlled, he never took to money-lending because his religion forbade it.

In 1901, AMJ had built a magnificent Bohra mosque in Mombasa at the cost of 50,000 rupees. Situated on a high cliff overlooking the Old Harbour, the three-storied building included cut stonework, ornamental plastering, coloured glass panes and exquisitely carved woodwork. It was large enough to comfortably accommodate the later increase in population but in 1982, forty-two years after AMJ's death, the Bohra priesthood razed it to the ground and Mombasa lost a major historical landmark.

However, one monument to AMJ still endures and that is Jeevanjee Gardens in the heart of Nairobi. In 1901, the British administration made plans for a public park to be included in Nairobi's development. They requested Delamere, who had been given vast areas of land virtually free, to donate a plot of his near the present Chester House in exchange for a site elsewhere. Delamere adamantly refused[22].

It was then that AMJ offered his land north of the Bazaar for the construction of the public park. He was an environmentalist who had earlier contributed to a public garden in Karachi and to the Treasury Square Garden in Mombasa. In the Nairobi park, he built a perimeter wall and put in two gates and several benches made of wrought iron. Being an admirer of Queen Victoria, he installed a statue of her on a pedestal and, with great foresight, laid down the proviso that the statue was never to be moved.

In 1906, the late Queen Victoria's son, the Duke of Connaught, unveiled the statue at a colourful ceremony. The park was named 'Jeevanjee Gardens' and became the property of the Town Council to manage and preserve for the citizens of Nairobi. The Gardens as we know them today are bare compared to their original state but the deterioration of the site is not just recent. As AMJ intensified his struggle against British injustice, the Settler-dominated Town Council opted to neglect the Gardens and by 1914, questions were being asked regarding the upkeep of the public park.

At a much later date the Gardens were partially rehabilitated. It is now a busy place, especially at lunchtime, used by office workers from the surrounding areas and by the itinerant preachers who ceaselessly compete for the attention of the crowd. Students and lecturers seek inspiration in the quiet shade and visitors to the city go there to rest their feet for a while. Over the years the Gardens has become a cultural melting pot; situated in the midst of a concrete jungle, it is a haven of peace where birds sing, trees bloom and green grass grows.

It is this 'haven of peace' that the Nairobi City Commission, in league with some shadowy developers, set out to destroy. The *Daily Nation* newspaper first exposed the plot to convert Jeevanjee Gardens into a parking lot and shopping mall on 24 June 1991. My mother Shirin Najmudean, AMJ's youngest child, and I mobilized forces to protest against this development. The Nation newspapers, Prof Wangari Maathai of the Green Belt Movement and concerned Kenyans supported the campaign. On 14 August 1991, President Daniel arap Moi ordered a halt to the development plans. Jeevanjee Gardens, was saved for the citizens of Nairobi.

In 1998, a Friends of Jeevanjee Gardens Society was formed to assist the Nairobi City Council to develop and improve the park. At the time of this writing, the condition of the Gardens has been much improved. Lockable gates and a perimeter fence ensure security and a full-time caretaker keeps the Gardens clean and tidy. Artistic seats and benches add to the aesthetics and a sculpture of Jeevanjee on a pedestal blends with the one of Queen Victoria installed in 1906. The long term plan of Friends of Jeevanjee Gardens is to develop the park into a lively square as an entertainment and socialisation centre thus reversing the tendency to inner city decay.

AMJ was a rare individual who sacrificed great wealth and status to fight for justice and equality. 'I look after my own interest but also I am always ready to yield to the higher interest of the public', he once stated. Even in the twilight of his life, AMJ's indomitable spirit remained resolute and despite the many betrayals, his financial collapse and political defeats, he did not become disillusioned. Seated on a rocking chair on the verandah of his house in Parklands, in spite of failing health, he would welcome visitors and discuss the latest local and international developments always urging them to keep up the struggle for equal rights. And as an enduring testimony he donated Jeevanjee Gardens, not just for the Indians of the Bazaar, but for all Nairobians. It is for us to ensure that his gift to posterity remains intact.

Endnotes

1. A. A. Engineer, *The Bohras*. Delhi: Vikas, 1980.
2. J. Jupp, (Ed). *The Australian People*. Australia: Angus and Robertson, 1988.
3. S. Jones, *Two Centuries of Overseas Trading*. London: The Macmillan Press Ltd., 1986.
4. *The Colonial Times*. November 1949
5. Kenya National Archives. *Testmonials of A.M. Jeevanjee & Co., Karachi & Mombasa.*
6. W. Rodney, *How Europe Underdeveloped Africa*. Nairobi: Heinemann, 1989.
7. *Kenya Daily Mail.* 18 May 1936.
8. R.G. Gregory, *India and East Africa*. Oxford: Clarendon Press, 1971.
9. Ibid.
10. Kenya National Archives, *East Africa Indian National Congress.*
11. H. Thuku, *Harry Thuku*. Oxford University Press: Nairobi, 1970.
12. R. G. Gregory, op.cit.
13. R. G. Gregory, Ibid.
14. Rhodes Library, Oxford. *Coryndon Papers.*
15. R. G. Gregory, op.cit
16. D. Seidenberg, *Uhuru and the Kenya Indians*. Delhi: Vikas Publishing House Pvt., 1983
17. *Kenya Daily Mail.* 7 May 1936
18. Kenya National Archives. AG 8/103
19. *The Times of East Africa.* 28 April 1906
20. Kenya National Archives. AG 23/241 & 258
21. Public Records Office, London. F0371/6003
22. E. Huxley, *White Man's Country*. London: Chatto & Windus, 1935.

Bibliography

Mangat, J.S. *History of the Asians in East Africa, 1886-1945*. Oxford: Clarendon Press, 1969.

Maxon, R.M. *Struggle for Kenya*, 1912-1923. London Associated University Press, 1993.

Oza, U.K. *The Rift in the Empire's Lute*,1900-1930. Bombay: (np, circa 1932-4).

Pandit, S. *The Indians in East Africa*. Nairobi: Panco Publications, 1961.

Patel, Z. *Challenge to Colonialism: The Struggle of Alibhai Mulla Jeevanjee for Equal Rights in Kenya* (Self published) 1997

Ross, W. M. *Kenya from Within*. London: George Allen & Unwin,1927.

www.ingramcontent.com/pod-product-compliance
Lightning Source LLC
Chambersburg PA
CBHW070742230426
43669CB00014B/2543